What it's like to feel

Jamie Cole

For Excerpts and Updates please follow:
Instagram.com/poetrybyjamiec
TikTok.com/poetrybyjamiec

ISBN: 979-8-218-39708-1

Book formatting and cover designed by Ravi

Acknowledgements

For my mom, the woman who has stuck by me, supported me through thick and thin, and always loved me unconditionally

For all my friends and family members who have read my poetry pieces over text message and motivated me to release this book

For anyone this might help or speak to

SPECIAL THANKS

*Ravi, who assisted with book formatting, provided publishing support,
and gave me permission to use their design on the book cover*

*Vee, who introduced me to Fiverr and helped
make publishing my book possible*

*Morgan and Nier, who inspired
my vision for the book cover*

TABLE OF CONTENTS:

Love 1

Heartache 39

Sadness 55

Hope.. 75

Love

Dancing lively
To beats of our own type of
drum

I hear memories
Replaying passion and lyrical
hums

Unforgettable reminders
Loop my mind from all of our
fun

While gazing
Inside your oceans reflecting the
sun

Savored flavors
Gift prizes which have never
been won

Flowers bloom
Inside my arms while embraced
in a hug

Sweetness rolls
Before biting into cones, off our
tongues

Peaks of interest
Illuminate paths, across streets,
as we run

Beginnings bright
Exploring what the future will
later behold

Swinging arms
Alongside the bass; down in
every bone

Visions, fleeting
Polarized pictures release by a
thumb

Admirable glimpses
Are captured between the
gasping of lungs

Acquired glasses
Borrow images from his eye's
lens for a second

Radiance shines
As her beauty develops after
instances mentioned

Warm snugs
With gore, loud and while
captions are shown

Pumping hearts
Sharing music, which to them,
feels like home

What can I say?
I like playing with matches

Rage spreading wildfire
Fire-taming with a passion

You push the smoke through my
lungs
And I can barely catch my
breath

Lit like the blunt
You ignite my heart
Using the same lighter you
sparked with

Sometimes love can fucking
burn
But between the blunt and your
lips
It never hurts for too long

Blasts like fireworks
Make it hard to look away
Love can be so beautiful

Holding me close in your arms
I can see the embers in your eyes
They reflect as the fire kindles
I won't ever leave your side

Warmth through our skin
The temperature rises, as the bed
shakes
Candles flare and so subtly flicker
As love is written through dim
lights

Like those first summer nights
A comforting heat grows within
This fondness, so highly
flammable
It's impossible to let it fade

Boiling in California weather
Sunshine becoming an escape
Your sunlight gleams down on
my skin
And nothing's ever felt quite the
same

Romantic pyros, we are
Butting our heads just like rams
This campsite has become our
home once again

Dripping sweat, by the pellet
stove
Exhaling of breath visibly
shown
At least we don't ever have to
worry about getting cold

Lost in your eyes
Not blinded, but unforeseen
I can't help but admire
Each piece of you, you've shown
me

Give in
Desperate to explore this
My mind can't resist you
Though it's even harder to
indulge in

Remind me
All I want is to see things
through
Constantly losing chances
Because I can never accept a
good thing when I'm left to

I'm vulnerable
With the heart of a coward
I have the potential to love you
I'm just scared I don't know how
to

I can't catch myself
Right below
You've got me

Under covers
In your arms
Where I'm supposed to be

How I've survived
Like this
I couldn't tell you nor do I want
to

Stuck on my mind
Irrational decisions
I wouldn't dare do

Less than a month ago
And yet,
You get where these ideas come
from

And, as hurtful as that is to
know
Shouldn't I be able to do this to?

Asking too much
But I can't disagree
I might need someone

No hesitation
No one I've ever known
Matters enough to rely on

I hope maybe one day
For you
My life becomes more feasible

Because as much as I want to
give you the world
That also means one that isn't
without me in it too

Call it wishful thinking
But I can't stop picturing
Reality harnessing imagery
Transmitted through dream
patterns, vividly

Holding dear to me, futuristically
Murals beyond frequencies
which visit me
What's coming next, envisioning
Travels commenced by accessing
mind's doors as they're opening

Though quickly, there's many
And for a matter of seconds,
only
Grasping, I can't help, embracing
Bounds rupturing and destroying
what once held me back from
exploring

Fate, restoring destiny
Taking shape as it should be
right before me
Immersions, mesmerizing
I reside here and know there's
really no other place I'm quite
meant to be

Alongside fear - love is fulfilling
Unsure what is or isn't, yet
known happily
This is who I am, supposedly
Worrisome, but at the same time
always so uplifting

Virtually, generating
Simulations I temporarily inhabit
are freeing though arguably
nonfactual on the surface

Everything, worth believing
This isn't fiction - my mind seeks
truth and speaks each word felt
now with purpose into existence

Sleepwalking while
picturing this future
Evolving in depths not
visible by eyes
Envisioning us together,
among them, forever

Years starting to dissipate
slowly, as is time
Omniscience displayed,
starting to convince me
Unable to be certain, bu
why spend life being afraid?

Lively, spunky - qualities
both of which are lovely
Accepting what's likely and
hoping internal doubts
contained will change

Teetering moments, such as
these, controlled
purposefully

Easing into opportunities
which align to form physically
Ready, to experience the
realities of their love often
described through the lines;
ready to experience them in
person - in real life

A poem
A song
It's been the small things all
along

Music booms
Water runs
After lathering myself in soap

My hands
Caress my breasts
Feeling almost as if you're here
touching my skin

Your voice
Echoes within
I want the sounds you
produce to surround me again

Smooth as the high noon
Softened up like butter

One night before
Right into another

Unanticipated
And yet, so all in its place

Alive, awake
And so very hard to contain

Until we meet again
I won't let these memories fade

Thank you for igniting this spark
I'll make sure to watch over the
flame

Satiated in bliss
Glad this moment wasn't lost

Thrilling from within
Endless, fleeting thoughts

Purposeful, thoughtful
Heart so open and exposed

You welcomed me in so subtly
Feeling good to be home

Hard not to question
Easier to accept these moments
as they come

Not quite put together
But nothing I need to prove to
you or anyone

Reminded my strength
Fluid as I go through these
motions

You take me as I am
Yet are constructive when giving
judgement

I could spill my heart on a page
Almost certain you'd read
through it

There isn't a need to hide
anymore
Accepted and encouraged

I don't know what could be
And there's no use rushing
things

But I'll return this spark back to
you
I'm just hoping I don't lose it on
the way

My minds been a little bit
clouded
With thoughts lacking
investment
And with even more about what
you might do with me next

I shouldn't want you but
temptations are hard to silence
I've never felt this wanted
without having to give anyone
reasons why I'm worth it

Lure me in for a taste, I long to
take the bait
I'd just like to know what it
could be like to let you guide me
for the night

Running my fingers through
your hair or down the inches of
your spine
Breathing me in, between the
lessons your tongue and lips
teach - soon you could be mine

I'd let you through and beneath
cotton seams
Take all that's within you, feel
some of it within me

I continue to hold onto the rush
that thoughts of you bring
I'm unable to let go of this way
we connected, you see

I didn't walk into your life to be
just another person who exits
Let me stay and I promise to
show you each reason you're
worth it

Accepting the ways, you've taken
a hold of my heart ever since
I wonder if it's okay for me to at
least keep these butterflies you
sent

The Garden of Eden
Flourishes throughout four
major seasons

Saplings, which rise
Above what our souls once
knew to believe in

Sprouting, exceeding
Limitations, we defy, just for the
sake of play

Beauty, out there
The sun gives directions so we
can pave our own way

Wilted, seasonally
We search for solace and water
for survival

Drenched, definitely
Down pours of rain wash over
and upon us

Growing, inspired
By mud sludge, dense grass and
backyards

Flowers, budding
Instinctually and with just all the
light in the world

Imagining your smile
Kicking my legs, jumping high
Belting, lyrics felt inside
Found me, you did
Across a mass of drowning eyes

Can't quite reach you now
A mirage I've painted, looking
beautiful
Twisting 'round and 'round
Thoughts, as reminders
Collide into me like usual

Throwing my arms to the sky,
laughing
They are unable to come down
Energy, radiating from my pores
Knowing, you're forever in my
company
Wanting more

My eyes would be stuck on you
In any natural state you exist
Your hands, moving downwards
Greetings, they'd make -
gripping tightly on my waist

Swaying, teaching
These words you haven't heard
and don't yet know
Searching, my eyes
While you guide my fingers in
towards your soul

Lingering, pictures of
What it would look like to have
you here next to me
Crazy to think you aren't actually
With you, again, I will be,
guaranteed

Tonight, with me, your essence
seeps from personified beats to
my shins
Into the floor, through the base
boards, vibrations march with
my stomping

Tossing myself; neck sore
Thwarting, my body side to side
Catapulting, near others
Pounding, basses boom at once
and they strike

My feet, smacking the ground
beneath me
Making contact; toppling
forward
Clumsily falling, doesn't happen
Sweating in your arms, I only
dream of

Holding still with time and
motivated by our propensities of
movement
Release; breaking into mixed
jitter dances from sudden
influence

Until our knees become weak
and our last ice cubes have
melted
All night long, as each song
arrives and plays on

Unison, we make occurrences
such as these ones, ones we
won't forget ever

Music as therapy, feet dancing
Hearts keep singing as their
beating

Submerged in riptides
Irises crashing, so rapid

Your raft keeps me afloat
Until diving deeper, so happens

Swimming, feeling natural
Though my arms flail with a
passion

Gracefully drowning, I sink
Good thing I'm a water
breathing master

Hanging onto hope
Taking things as they come
Wearing a smile
Daydreaming beyond what's
comfortably numb

Circulations, timed
Alongside my heart's beating
unrest
Cardiac rhythms
Transmit centrally to extremity
tips

Warmth, radiating
Through cheeks flushing red
Extensions stretch
Imagined embrace, relieves
tension known by my chest

Salt streams, releasing
A leakage of happiness from
sight
Never alone
Reminders of what's true within,
feeling right

Venturing horizons
Wandering, inside the unknown

Tempting secrecy
Curiosity, prevails me to go

Sights unforeseen
Distinctive and delightfully felt

Embodied stability
Soaring space with a gravity belt

Associations new
Exploring realms discreetly in
pleasure

Explosive energy
Pervasive; exceeding desirable
measure

Illusive exposure
Vibrant, grounding reels me
back home

Passions delicate
Admirations, meaningfully
fostering growth

Beauty is more than a shaved
body and clean skin

Beauty is the essential oils in my
hair and sweat dripping from the
gym

Beauty is spinach between my
teeth and eggs benedict flavored
breath

Beauty is the natural aroma
along my neck, arms, and legs

Beauty is the way I taste and
smell after just waking up

Beauty is relaxing on the couch
with a smile and some musk

Beauty is applied using makeup
brushes or without any effort at
all

Beauty is brown eyes and brown
hair - like the leaves in the fall

Beauty is an hourglass, perky tits,
and a handful of ass

Beauty is hair wrapped up or
flowing down my soft, slender
back

Beauty is untamed eyebrows and
mud facial masks

Beauty is freckles on my face
and my shoulders to match

Beauty is sweatpants, wearing
nothing, or dresses almost to
short

Beauty is everything I am and all
of the sorts

Shared thoughts
Appreciation

Fascination
Interests peaked

Pinch myself
Immersed in daydreams

Night-seeking
Not asleep

Bliss
Felt inside echoes

Happiness heard
In words which you speak

Souls, weep
Heart liquids, seep

Love, so deep
And surely meant to keep

Embodiments
Which ascend

Making
Almost too much sense
No end
Apparent

Beginnings, cycle
Cycling again

Synchrony
On repeat

Insightful unison
Now blends

Complimenting
One another

Blooming
In memories we spend

Pieces taking
New formations

Excitable patterns
Heavensent

Assembled parts
Made to fit

Eyes stream
Dispersions fill the rest
Explorations, taken
Lingering in labyrinths of depth

Curiosity, shining
Illumination embroidered well
within

Visionaries
Project vibrations

Desired passion
Expels your chest

Unbeknownst
Before we met

Lost in seconds
Timely spent

Hardwiring, enjoyed
Nuance streaming out from your
lips

Thoughtful, neural firing
Inspires how your energy
transmits

Gratefully, observing
Delicacies releasing well from
your mind

Mental circuitry, gleaming
Expressions cherished for all of
their kind

Defying gravity
In melodies, we're flowing

Endlessly, terrestrially
In galaxies, we're floating

Space travel, exploring
In minds, thoughtfully roaming

Cosmically, driven
In pleasantries, eternally
knowing

Stars fill vision fields
Dark matters becoming placed

Bright vocal emissions
Illuminate our ears with new
taste

Rotations, creations
Comets spew courage beyond
text

Foreign planets, they spin
Hopping between moons to the
next

Beautifully, universal
Effortless hopes, requiring time
first

Rockets, lift off internally
Artificially unique, intelligently
diverse

Caught in your orbit
Divine and most certainly drawn
right to

Constellations of phrases
Forces building only with
intentions for you

Butterflies
Tickle the inside of her stomach

Blushing
Cheeks, warm, like summertime
sunsets

Jitters
He still tends to make her feel a
bit nervous

Soft smooches
Her mind revisits memories,
enjoyed, for a moment

Hoping
He'll want to stay here, beside
her, a little while longer

Gazing
Not as shy, her lips outline her
now open-mouth smile

Electrifying
His pull persuades her face to
lean back into his, closer

Insatiable
Her lips, again, lust at the
thought of tender kiss hunger

While observing you
Peaceful in slumber
My mind races
As I ponder
What the future holds

In this moment
It feels like I've been given the
world
If only to smile
And be my authentic self

Living, without bounds
I find comfort in this skin
This skin in which, I've made
into my home
And which you hold

The little things
Often serve as gentle reminders

Of time spent, smiling
And, at times, when life's feeling
brighter

Neglecting clock hands
We blend our sentences with
tears and our laughter

Luminescent, our love glows
And is savored together now and
thereafter

Wishing calls never ended
While soaring beyond lines of
transmitted waves

Some days, feeling quite strange
Until we speak and return to
pathways we've paved

Being with you, like a dream
state
Forgetting sadness in me exists

Your voice, feeling like home
Grounding me to mental states
I'd rather live in

Distance, never-ending
Realities we live are currently
separate, it's true

Work left to be done
Most days, it's on me, to self-care
and self-soothe

Never alone, though it seems
Moments are ones I pursue by
myself, on my own

Nothing is ever lost
And soon, we can return back to
bloom and can grow

Appreciation beyond compare
Though we do not speak as
often
I never stop thinking of you

The strongest I've known
With titanium bones
Far surpassing
He exceeds anyone

Worries but always keeps it
together
Charismatic
Adores me for everything I am
And for that I am lucky

There is not a thing I would
change
Or a thing I would do differently
I wouldn't want a man to change
himself for me

Comfortable in his skin
Meditative, despite voices in his
head
An attraction like no other

I've stopped craving other
bodies
Because sex with anyone else
would be meaningless

A voice that lifts me up
Even with all this distance
physically
I love you, always
I love you, endlessly

Cadences alike
Surpassing all that I've known

Understanding matched
Vocalizations welcome me home

Comforting, somber
Hopes to stay just a little bit
longer

Separation, mindful
Apart while always together

Lifting above
The sky, parting open before me

Thoughtfully realizing
Loving, deeply and congruently

Embracing decay
Hearts stir crazed, night until day

Until next time
In my mind, which you will stay

Do I have your attention?
If so, how do I keep it?

Unsure what you're thinking
Although, maybe it's best kept a
secret

Elevated like a queen
Gasoline fueling the rush in my
body

Words spelled out from the
scrabble
Could help dissolve what now is
foggy

Is this something you're feeling,
too?
Or, is it just me?

Without the present distance
between
Maybe, it would be easier to see?

Situations played out differently
Chances to connect visually
feasible

Possibilities becoming reality
Requests for your time much
more achievable

Cannot forget that goodbye
A kiss while being lifted off my
feet

You left me questioning
If, perhaps, events were unique
to just me
A late-night burrito
5am conversations, laughing in
your car

Sharing songs and stories
Compliments of my beauty
while staring at stars

Romantically, processing
What things represented and
might mean

Solve this puzzle for me
I'm currently curious about what
could be

No wrong answers, of course
Leaving this conversation causal
and open

You said actions shown were not
like you
And passion has fed desires
worth holding

Enjoying spontaneity
Freedom of expectations and
stress

Comfortable in intimacy
Feeling each restless moment
with bliss

Though, I still can't help but
wonder
Whether you introduce every girl
you've just met to close friends?

I'll try not to get hung up on
Answers to thoughts which are
likely better left in my head

Effortless, feeling
Reaching to grasp, bliss
Love, and with comforts
Long sought after, before this

Lucky, as I'm seeing
Imaginable, though creatively
couldn't
My mind never knew, brilliance
Until it was you, which I met

Half a year ago
I would not have been able to
say what true love is
Or should feel like
But I can now, so that's all okay

Mirages, deceptive
I previously painted pieces
without attempting to perfect
my own vision
Never grabbing tones that
piqued my interest
Or, trying new strokes in the
moment

Rough drafts
Fulfillment I now receive from
my revisions
Entries, I love, continue
While others collect dust in my
closet

Moving on to brighter and better
things
I'm starting to understand
Some stories just become less
appealing

And some chapters in new
books are started before ever
reaching one's endings

Realizing it's acceptable to put
books down if I don't like them
Deciding to keep reading
Reading, what speaks to me
And only if I enjoy what I'm
feeling as I do so

I may have never been here
If not for the spark you ignited
Ignited and fueled, by chaotically
raging hearts
I would not give up this book
for anyone or anything else

Trying to find
The right way to describe
How something seemingly
minuscule
Could make me feel this alive

Unexpectedly found
Mentally, not all quite there
Definitely wasn't expecting
To find such acceptance, so rare

Difficulty, placing my thoughts
Nervous, because you're so
lovely
Tangled in knots, wondering
If you'd take the chance to just
know me

Rambunctiously jumbled
Overlapping maps routed inside
Create syntactic connections
So, it's possible, they'll reach you
in time

My heart as my guide
If you wanted, you could
borrow my eyes
Then you'd see the draw you
have
Your welcoming smile; sweet
and divine

How sun rays glowed off your
skin
Peaking behind your bodies
outline
Crystallized irises seeking amber
Colliding currents meet with
cavernous kinds

Ahead of myself, maybe
Call me goofy, a bit crazy
Undeniably interested in mystery
Embarking life's journey,
persistently

Enjoying company, our laughter
Time to converse and vibe on
the road as we ride
Similarities, fun, and attractions
aside
Let's take a drive so I can learn
how to surf in your tide

Wanting nothing more
Than to show you affection
Tender, soft kisses
Inhaling your breaths, in

Breaking barriers
To entry ways which relieve
every tension
Temperatures rise
Passionate desires, all worth the
mention

Please describe for me, how
You'd break this back of mine
right in two
Sinister - when delivered
Pieces, resembled by you once
moments ring true

Lying flat on my stomach
My face, pushed upon a mattress
of springs
Bed shakes mirror movements
made
As manifestos play and pluck my
heart strings

Indulging what inside
Festers greater longing and
waiting
Encapsulations of hope
Beyond caverns stretching and
fiending

Devour my heart
Spitting out chunks which are
harder to swallow
Lick my bouquet filled with
daisies
Until rivers leaking rapid, run
hollow

Delicacies of flavor
Tasted between soft passages of
flesh
Overflowing with mastery
Through inviting doors, open
and spread

Really wanting nothing more
Than to show you affection
Embracing what my mind says
Envisioning what we'd do if we
only had just a second

Seduction you speak, persuades
Garments of my clothes to fall
off

Hunger, builds up within me
And leaves my body begging for
more

Craving passion, you paint
Fantasizing your soft touch on
my skin

Elevations of bliss
Illustrate realities of truth on
repeat in my head

Imagery behind eyelids
I wander comfortably in the
sound your voice

Gliding fingertips
Across my skin plains until
deeper by choice

Fucking, synchronized poetically
Firmly grasping devotions
mentally kept

Filthy thoughts, cinematically
Convey perfect emissions you've
sent

Hypnotic, trances
Flow through me slowly and
take over my essence

Gasping for air
Spellbinding I plead to feel all of
your indulgence

While aimless and searching to
feel whole
Light found me wandering down
the darkest of tunnels

Time, these days, spent soaring
above clouds in the skies
The true meaning of happiness
now floats along with me at my
side

Dream states pave realities for
me as I wake
What appears wrong on the
surface only feels right in my
brain

My life, once spent secretly
drowning alone out at sea
No longer requires flailing and
sinking, but instead helps me
breathe

Self-control slowly escaping me,
I don't mind and with reason
The ones here who support me
show love while they question
my thinking

Impulse, this inner vice, I
embrace in my heart and my
soul
Undeniably, pushes me towards
what I want and seek most

No intentions to forfeit love I
have, not now or not ever
Desire compels me to proceed
on this sweet, sweet endeavor

Imagery of a future foggy, and
yet, appearing always in reach
I have trust in my fate and what
the mirror lets me see

Demolishing parts I've built,
only to rebuild them more stable
Forces tell me to flee, and I
have hope I will live a life more
worthwhile

This could be the end of me,
and I've accepted what around
me must change
As everybody around me paints
me as an enemy - mad and so
strange

Only temporary obstacles, as I
rise and bask in our bliss
Opportunities endless and a life
I surely won't miss

Events I could have never
expected; grateful as I am lucky
I've come so far and with you is
all I could ever wish to be, truly

Looking at you
Means seeing
Crystallizing oceans
Below 0 degrees Celsius

Looking at you
Means melting
Through cracks
Of iris fixed crevices

Looking at you
Means calming
Relaxed eyebrows
Resting above your eyelids

Looking at you
Means smelling
Musky scents
Mixed with your deodorant

Looking at you
Means tasting
Words leaving
Between our lips into my
esophagus

Looking at you
Means remembering
Luminance, radiant
As my blood warms beneath my
lightened skin

Looking at you
Means lacing
Fingers round'
Each hair attached to your skull

Looking at you
Means touching
Soft noses
And gazing beyond sights we
only dream of

Looking at you
Means caressing
Loving hands
To each other's cheeks combined
with cravings to be held

Looking at you
Means feeling
Eternal bliss
Before pressing our lips -
as we close our eyes and lean in

HEARTACHE

What do you want me to say?
That I want to scream at you and
tell you you're being an asshole
That I'm literally scared to be
near you and scared of what shit
you're going to say about me
next?
That I feel like I'm on egg shells
because I don't know what thing
I'll do to trigger your anger
again?
That all I really want right now
is to not look at you or speak to
you until you get everything off
your chest?

I never envisioned it was
possible for me to view my
partner this way
But it feels like it's so easy for
you to let out your rage when
you want to
It's like most times you're angry
you don't have any concern
for what you say or how it may
affect me or my emotions

Why do I even care as much as
I do?

Why do I shove these disgusting
thoughts down and swallow my
pride for you when it's perfectly
okay for you to hurt me when
you want to?

Maybe we should just argue with
each other till our hearts are
content?
See who can have the last word
and see how many hurtful things
we can think of next?
If you want this relationship to
be toxic, you're leading things
down that path

I never even could think of how
to ask or make some of the
comments you have made - and
now I can
I'm not okay with this
I'm not okay with having this
anger in me
It's not who I am
I hate with everything inside me
that I could even intentionally
think of how to get back at you
or hurt you
I cannot bear to live this way

If I talked to you the same ways
you are to me now or some of
the other times you have in the
past, you'd stand up for yourself
You'd use your voice and say
what's on your mind without a
second thought
The minute I say something
even remotely off from my sad
or jovial tones, you bark at me
for having an attitude

I'm trying not to act off my
emotions
I'm not trying to make myself
all big and tall and say some
pointless shit I don't need to
It's just very hard when you're
never afraid to
When you're pressing an issue
and poking at me constantly to
"spit it out"

You can say "I don't listen for
shit" and feel nothing about it
Tell me to "grow up", say
"boohoo", or give me shit
But me wanting to call you an
asshole makes me wish I didn't
have the urge to or even the
thought to in the first place

Why are you so okay with doing
it?
I thought I was the person you
were in love with

I don't want the anger you have
inside you but slowly I feel my
blood starting to boil
This rage inside me when you
talk under your breath or tell me
what to do when I have my own
agenda mapped out perfectly
fine
The patience you often lack
when I'm just trying to do my
best
Like what the fuck is your issue?

You can say it was how you were
raised all you want but what's my
excuse?
Do you want me to start
expressing my anger and tell you
this heat pent up within me is
because of you?

I've never been the type to let
my anger out this way
Normally, I just let it pass and
drift away without letting a word
out of my mouth
I move on because it doesn't
ever accomplish anything helpful

Lately all I want to do is fucking
shout
But I'm a sensitive bitch so what
would that even solve?

I'm not okay with being your
punching bag just because you
don't know how to treat people
when you're frustrated
And I'm not okay with being
spoken to some of the ways you
have when you're in a negative
headspace

Either start training those types
of comments out from your
mind or learn how to at least
keep some of these comments
to yourself

Because next time you feel the
need to direct something rude at
me, I'm done
I'm going to explode

This is me warning you now I
don't know the type of person
you're making me become
But she's pissed, unhinged, and
the least bit predictable

Waking up to find
What's unforgivable in your eyes

Wishing I meant more
Than these words that you speak

Desperately seeking revival
Pain now lingers in my chest

Through what's blurry
I type in darkness as I weep

Far surpassing
Any individual I've been able to
know

I cannot imagine
Not being beside you as we
continue to grow

Fragile pieces
Assemble redemption and to
again become whole

Hoping to gift
Down the line, trust to a heart
made of gold

Mirroring each other
A harmony of complimentary
opposites

Yin and Yang
Nothing could ever break or
even stop us

Tapestries of beauty
Made from fabric and these

stories untold

Constructed passions
Fostered by needles while
reaping what's sewn

One can only hope
A glimmer sits in this pit filled
with darkness

Bracing for anything
Desiring nothing more than to
just keep on and fight this

Everything on the line
Doing anything that could ever
be wanted

Dissociative living
I yield words that are nothing
but honest

A smile, luminous
Envisioning greatness cheek to
cheek on its own

Understanding you must do
What you need and is best for
your soul

For you, either way
I speak my intentions to soften
the blow

Take what's left
Of what within me, apologizes
and feels everything so deeply so

1:28pm
While roaming the aisle of stores

Checking the time
Her heart grows cold from all of
the sores

Good morning texts
Realizing, these, she will no
longer see

Understanding why
It was easier for him to end
things and leave

Disconnected
He builds walls from a monster
which feeds

Unable to fix it
Living with pain of what won't
ever be

People who are kind
Deserve more than a dishonestly
beast

Without consideration
Decisions, haunting, can close
now and cease

Hyper-focusing
Spilling poems upon a telephone
screen

Rereading words
Hope dims, becoming dark -

without any gleams

Barbed wire hands
Oh, how she bloodied the heart
he wears on his sleeve

The doors closing
Earlier, while shoppers prepare
for Thanksgiving feasts

Sitting aimless
Alone, saddened, in the car -
desperate in need

2:47pm
Accepting these words, he'll
likely never read or receive

I imagined
Receiving flowers
Not crying in my shower
About expectations I thought
were enough

Most actions of yours
I appreciate, yes
But nothings warmer than your
touch and your love

The days you decide
Affection comes second
Remind me of moments I felt
lost, years before

To be smothered in kisses
Are nothing but visions
From a time I once loved, now
nothing more

It's easy becoming haunted
When you lose your place
And are forgotten
Deprived, of what you've
wanted all along

I'm starting to believe
Investment is a daydream
The result of me expecting too
much and wanting more

I don't always feel this way
But, in moments, I'm reminded
Being brushed off makes me
feel so utterly small

Disposed and confused
Thoughts, like untended wounds
The hurt pours out and I can't
make it stop

You know where it hurts
In more places than one
And yet, my sentences are
crumpled and then tossed

I'm tired of asking
And confessing my thoughts
When in the end, they'd get
ignored from the start

Love, equates differently
Unmatched in empathy
Conversations, first hollow then
trail off

An apology feels owed
I'd rather shower alone
I really wish it meant something
to you when I spoke

A peace I thought I'd never find
This peace, it's mine

As you piece me back together
"They're just thoughts; you're
fine."

The type of love that's never
taken
Given away; then rightfully
returned

It surprises you - at every turn
A comfort that is thrilling; up,
down
And yet, still almost feels
undeserved

I've never been this scared to
lose someone in my life
But somehow I destroy the
bridge over to you
Each and every time

I become satiated in our bliss
Smothered and not at all
concerned
Easy to latch onto this comfort
Quick to let it burn

The toxicity rolls off the tip of
my tongue
Oblivious, and now slowly we're
losing touch
We're too far gone for me to bite
down now
The damage has been done

My efforts are no longer enough

Our hands, once intertwined,
start losing grip
Through the cracks, our love
begins to slip

The peace has been broken
Vulnerable and exposed
The heart once on your sleeve,
lies ripped open on the floor

I need to stop keeping tally's
Because at odds end, who cares
about the score

How do I assemble our love
back together?
Patch by patch, I beg that maybe
I can make it whole

Despite my overall best
intentions and the inexcusable
actions I project
I just know, I feel peace when
I'm with you
You're not something I'm
prepared to forget

I need to stop giving you reasons
to leave me
This time we can make love -
not war

But most importantly, I'm sorry
And I promise I won't let myself
hurt you anymore

Russian
Roulette
Except imagine the barrel is full

Aiming
At me
He places his sights on my skull

Releasing
Bullets
Fascination grows from my
obstruction

Speech
Firing
Blood leaking disrupts cortical
function

Wounds
Pour
As I fear making additional
mistakes

Executions
Flawless
If his motive was to go through
my brain

My mind
Pierced
He pulls the trigger after each
word he says

Destruction
Caused
From ways I, too, shoot myself
to feel pain

Inflicting
Harm
Is how I manage my hurt as it's
flowing

Projecting
Frustration
He contributes to hate inside
which is growing

Wishing
My partner
Now, prioritized healing over my
suffering

Disappointing him
Often
Due to my tendencies of
forgetting

Sufficiently
Powered
Knowledge is then used to try
killing me slowly

No longer
Sacrificial
I do not ever wish to die for him
willingly

Why does he despise me?
And desire me upon the floor,
dead

"Close your lips, please," I said
"Stop speaking and stop taking
shots at my head."

I can't help but feel
The hate you hold in your heart
Isn't also hate, in me
You've felt since the very start

I don't know, how to accept
What you vocalize to me
Could be out of genuine
curiosity
Just as much as it could be out
of insult or to pass judgement

Navigating, with open stitches
I haven't discovered how to see
Purity in your intentions
When speaking on who I am
and the ways I've only ever
understood how to think

Me, what it means to be me as a
person
Is to never feel like something
"matched" with you in
comparison

The individual, I am, when it
comes to you
Continues to feel like one which
never stops being in competition

I haven't determined how to win
or end this yet
Though both outcomes are ones
I can say I never wanted to begin
with

In many aspects, which you
stand by
I haven't come to terms with
how
Deviations in ways I experience
the world
And ways I choose to live could,
too, themselves be just as fine

Inclined, to hide
More than I wish to express
what sits on my mind
Words you speak typically feel
painful
And the worst part is, I can't
quite shake or put my finger on
why

Historically, it was acceptable
At this point, it could be false
but still is not easy to detach
from

Lack of progress that once was
present is supposedly not now
Though it remains uneasy
To see through a lens that
doesn't to you view me as
anything other than incompetent

I can't help but always feel I'm
falling short to you
Not falling close enough for you
Something clearly not enough
for you
And something not ever really
measuring up for you

Feeling like I will to you,
continue being what you view as
Damaging or in ways lacking
What to you, I've only wished
Wasn't a way it was ever possible
for you to view me

Difficulty responding
I latch onto old perceptions
When you, before, wanted to
diminish me on purpose
Though you say that's no longer
the truth behind your actions
It's not something I've been able
to forget has happened

Because then, I wasn't worthy
Then, I only deserved to be
What makes now unlike the rest?
How does it so happen to not be
true anymore?

Maybe I was and always have
been?
And just didn't notice I
should've been treated at all
differently
Either way, I haven't mastered
a way to see beyond these
portrayals of what, from that
time, have since stuck with me

33 voicemails
And a number of missed calls

None, from you though - ever
I'm lucky if I get to hear from
you at all

Trying to keep my head on
straight
Fighting, it spins instinctually on
a swivel

Echoes vibrate through minds
walls
Noise seeping between the
cracks lying all but in the middle

I forget to care, then in seconds
it'll hit me
Abruptly, flooded with a
reminiscent bliss, mixed with
envy

Beginning to question what
I might mean to you in this
moment, yet again
But at the same time, why does
this even matter to me anyway?

Sentences trail off, as to be
expected
In all honestly, what do I truly
ever have to go off of?

Stimulated, enticing - take things
as they are - inviting
The heart grows fonder as it
continues beating from inside
me

Offerings made beyond past
comforts
Overthinking in this situation
seems to stunt my flow

There's not a threat to be seen
Yet perceiving it stands waiting
at the end of the hall - it's
distracting

Am I being just plain cruel?
Or am I at least pleasantly
deceitful?

Calculating, I try to decipher this
problem
Though I don't really know if it's
something that needs solving

Relax, have fun
What do I really have to lose?
Come on

Live for your own contentment
Remind yourself if he had an
issue he'd tell you

I wrack my mind on this rainy
Sunday in my cubical
I hold onto the pieces of
happiness you gave me this
morning to grasp

Cherishing the frill and what is
soothing in your melodies once
more
I'll practice taking my strides
a bit slower and accept the
possibility this might not last

Though not audio impaired
I stomp my feet around like a
bear
Living freely, lacking decency
Does that make me evil for not
taking consideration of others
before my actions?

Being respectful to others in the
home
The expectation which feels
owed and requires me to shift
how I perform tasks and close
passages

But I wonder if one day,
clanking around my kitchen sink
didn't actually have to mean so
much to anyone else
If the way I lived life didn't
require change or any ounce of
scrutiny

If I could close the cupboards a
little too loud
Sometimes
All the time
Every time
And whether it startled you,
made you laugh, or made you
and the kids think "oh yeah,
that's just mom out there. She
can be a bit loud sometimes."

You would love me for me, not a
drop less
All the same, always

Endearing, non-judgmental
As if how I chose to live didn't
require any fixing
Like I had flaws, but they were
worth bearing because they were
not horrible to begin with

Seriously, I'm fucked up but
All I really needed was a little
mentoring was all

Courage that my faults didn't
make me any less beautiful
Knowing the bad things which
come with what you did like,
didn't have to be so disturbing
to you

Bothersome enough to drill into
me
To the point it starts shifting
your thinking

Did you think I wanted to be
this much of a sore in your side?
This aspect of life that, no
matter how hard it tries, only
continues to keep losing luster in
your eyes

Realizing this is the life I chose,
though I continue to wonder
what for
I thought it was what I wanted,
back then I suppose so

Not having to live any particular
way for you is what I wish now
At that time, I wanted only to be
consumed but now I don't want
to be anymore

SADNESS

Lurking from the shadows
Wickedly silent, she entered

Gripping a hold of my neck
For mere entertainment, she
chuckled

Suffocated with chloroform
She rendered my body
unconscious

Taking over this vessel
She left her mark while playing
with fondness

Anticipated, it wasn't
Swept over my eyes - such
compulsions

Sobbing in the mirror
Is this me or am I just watching?

Lifeless, with a pulse
Drag these legs across the whole
city

Though all I wanted last night
Was departure from my reality

What happens in here
Halfway intentional, half only
the thought of

On the surface, she looks pretty
Pretty depressed, though entirely

She wears the smile so well
Discreetly, as if, there's somehow
a secret

To enjoying a life on the surface
While wanting nothing more
than to end it

You couldn't tell she was
running
Running low and on empty

The facade of the century
Laughing, admiration by all in
her beauty

It's a lie though, you know
As hard as she tries to please
everyone

It could happen at any moment
She's just not sure yet when her
time will come

Fixated
My focus begins shifting
As I put on my glasses
Life's image becomes clearer
And yet, I still can't equate a
meaning

Dull
Like an unsharpened pencil
It's physically there
As I hold this tangible object, in
hand
Ultimately, it's remains dull
because the point is still missing

Days start feeling less appealing
Reality blends and fills all the
gaps in between
Consuming the majority of days,
I spend
Enjoyment starts to feel
imagined

You mean to tell me people just
wake up
And allow themselves to live
lives that make them happy?
And yet I'm still stuck in a world
of thinking
That does nothing but destroy
me?

I say stuck as if I don't have the
ability to fix this
Even as I'm in full bloom
A new leaf; sometimes a bud
Just the right amount of water
to grow
And somehow, undoubtedly
consumed

As if the sun I need is not
hitting me the right way and
there's just something I'm not
getting
Enough sun to mean something
Enough sun to really be getting
anything out of this life
Enough sun to truly show me
I'm changing and that I matter

Light
The tunnel is supposed to lead
here
But no one ever says how long
this tunnel is
How much time or energy it
takes to reach the end
Or if I'm even strong enough
for the journey

Why does my tunnel never end?
More like, why haven't I been
able to reach the end yet?

The people who know there's
light only know because they've
made it
It leaves me wondering if the
chance I had went unclaimed
and was regifted

Purpose
In the actions I put towards
others
Never amounts enough within
myself
To be worth serving
Or to fill this abyss of emptiness
that's felt

These are not even my late-night
thoughts
The kind that leave you restless
Preventing most from sleeping

These are what I carry around
on my back throughout the day
And lay to the floor
As I climb into bed for sleep
Soundly, in my escape

Thoughts I can't quite shake
I wish I could just put each one
into words for you
Instead, I waste hours thinking
of what to write
And end up making you wait
longer than you want to

It feels dramatic to say the least
That I still let these thoughts
consume me
Repetitive and relentless
Right on the tip of my tongue
but my doubtful mind stops me
from speaking

Most times they mean nothing
and are ultimately there to hurt
me
Quick to erase this progress I'm
making
Falsely believing I could do this,
and it'd be easy

Without a question you are here
for me and have good intentions
So why can't I let these things
go?
Why can't I flip a switch and
think clearly

Block this flow of negativity so
more positivity can flow through

Often drawing off deceptions of
what my life could become
There's no reason to think this
way anymore
There's so much more to look
forward to than my mind ever
gives my life credit for

Self-sabotaging and withdrawing
from the me I long to know
I need to stop fighting these
demons
They aren't mine anymore

You see the pieces of me
scattered
Time and time again
Trying to put me back together
I just wish it could be easier
Than constantly rebuilding this
puzzle

Vibrant hues
Pierce behind clouded skylines
Waves crash
As the moon caresses the
ocean's unwind

While gazing at tides
And enjoying night skies
Intrusive thoughts strike me,
tonight
About how I could die

"How I could", I notice
Does not assume me to at all be
"wanting"
Existing, they are
But doesn't mean I am
"planning" or "trying"

Methods, potentially
Ways of "how" often appearing
in my head
Understanding, anything is
possible
Death - without a guaranteed
end

Ideation and likelihood
Living along separate spectrums
I unravel the intricacies of my
seeing
Without any additional intention

Vividly,
I pictured myself walking
straight to the ocean
From third person, confident
Dead of night, slow motion

Flailing,
Life pans to a scene of me
drowning
My arms, abusing liquid surfaces
Colliding, ruptured seas
We battle, until what lives and
breathes ceases

Wondering what this feeling is
Becoming nothing while being
everything

Conversations, shift audibly
As silence in my head is
observed noticeably
I listen to other's words and hear
the currents pass me

The river rotations flowing -
peacefully
I do as they do and keep going

Dragged to nature's bath by
something within
Beyond my ankles
Rising from my bellybutton to
my ribs
Immersed, my shoulders covered
Water touches the tips of my ear
lobes

I recognize a decision was made
by me to dip my feet in
The funny thing is, I don't
remember making it

As I write now, I'm on land
Standing on rocks in sunshine

Reflecting, on this instance
which recently brought me
inward
Motivating my expression
I describe here what I saw while
watching murky water dance

Rippling, across my lenses
My eyes were met with a vision
close to my waterline
In awe and with the resolution
of waves heightened
I focused on each one as it
surged across
Thousands upon thousands of
tides visibly synchronized
Simultaneously and suddenly,
they made entry to my mind

I zoomed in deeper, an
appearance of black dots was
presented
Water spiders, I discovered, tiny
but their motions were still close
enough to be experienced
One, then two
My eyes began to zoom further
and further outward
Multiplying by the second, I
started seeing many more of
them
Existing at home together

Each of them gliding across the
surface in a different pattern
Their swimming, peculiar
And so vastly different from the
way the wind was whispering to
the water

Here, but not really
Moving with the river, and bugs,
raising to stand statically
My hands instinctively reached
forward to guide me as my torso
stumbled backwards, behind me

Life, being lived but also viewed
in modes cinematically
Large, slippery rocks changing
my feet's trajectory
My seat, jagged and coated in
mossy goo
I'm lucky the impact did not
hurt and introduced me to the
river's view

Outstretched, I raised my legs
Levitating near the bounds of
water and air
I rotated my palms up
While doing yoga, I began to
think about what it is this world
has in store for me?

Shuffling, I am thankful the
world allowed me to leave my
mind briefly
Unknown, and yet, not fearing
I understood that in a few hours
I would again feel it

Once I was no longer numb
And unable to be distracted
I would be left to feel what
internally, has my stomach
constantly stirring
Everything while being nothing
would stop being felt as
pleasantly

In search of a creative flow, I
don't seem to have one right
now
What I do know is I need to
grapple with what inside I
currently have no control over

Triggering, when nothing at this
point feels honest
Like my mind trips, I've fallen
into a deep abyss I can't get
myself out of

Empty words do their best to fill
me with hope temporarily
Each time, with sincerity,
and tied to beliefs it will play
differently

Although I've accepted and
comprehended I've moved on
from what him and I used to call
this
It's still just as difficult to
not give things in my life any
chances for improvement

Every situation adds more salt to
the wound
Gushing, never closing - burns
lack comfort and they loom
Feeling jabs to my heart when he
doesn't keep his word

It becomes exhausting hearing
excuses, and it has grown hard
to trust a promise's worth
Wishing desperately to come
first for even a day and that such
a thing was not something I ever
needed to convey

Always requested by me
when upset or something that
explicitly needs to be stated
when frustrated
Is this an issue with me?
Is wanting to feel in the center
of a person's world for a day
such a big ask?

Placement of myself there, not
feeling like something he wants
I want to be wanted
By him, it used to be something
I wanted

Occupied, my rumination
shouldn't be the reason I cry and
struggle so often
I am wanted, just clearly not
enough by him
It's obvious
That's fine, I do believe and
recognize that

Playing the part, I realize how
different my life is and will be
once it's able to be
This suffering, now, at one
point won't be my reality

Fighting for love also will no
longer be what I live for
Today, with a mixture of
spite, I feel inclined to pick
me, because I choose to

When he's "ready" to give me
his time again, I'll let him know
he missed his shot, already
3 hours ago "We'll need to
reschedule when you can hold
up your end," I'd tell him
Which feels like it will never
happen but could still feel
powerful to say

Falsely, he told me that we were
going to spend the day together
and asked me to not make plans

The truth is, I could be
somewhere else now
Connecting with the love of my
life or my friends

Promises lacking consistency,
they leave his lips and somehow
I wonder why I'm still so stupid

Lacking any real substance
Believing, my existence to him
isn't something always up for
auction or is beyond second best

Needless to say, I'm fed up
I'm worth more than what he
devotes
I'm over expecting it to change,
because it's not going to

Time to shape up my attitude
and instead, let go of hope

Victim to habit
Back to the same thoughts and
madness
Once locked, she's unleashed -
crazy, like bat shit
You'd look me in the eyes and
think "woah is she really like
this?"
Discerning, what among me is
sunshine or darkness

Concerning, the makeshift
energy and levels transcribing
Unmatched yet combusting a
little less passive
Parallels between what lies
within and beneath all the lines
Did you really think what lies
inside was something visible
outside?

Was it easier to believe she's soft
and lacking internal conflict?
Could I show you? Would you
like to come see it?
Would it be worthwhile to you?

Constantly I wonder, how I
got this far with a head full of
questions
Is it okay if I place them here
with you for a second?

Mumbling, when I express them
but fluently inside I speak
Free flowing, purposefully -
none of which is surprising
A big smile, falsely portrays a life
which isn't worth living
Wanting so hard to go beyond
written words which are hidden

Arm cramping, with how quickly
I release these down
Am I doing a good, proper job
at getting all of this out?
Will I ever be able to manage the
amo I speak of?
Is it at all a worry to anyone else
this is the calling I answer?

She's not okay, she isn't well
She's trapped in her own
personal hell
She hates herself and continues
to dwell
To anyone, why would she dare
ever tell?

Viewing reality from a different
perspective
Almost feeling like I'm outside
of this present dimension

1st person, lost - no longer
grounded to the seat I sit on
I notice shifting in my eyes,
fleeting, then my minds gone

Nothing; I see life in current
ways which are not my own
Peripherally, inept – yet
internally, I still roam

Dissociation from locations
which to me were previously
known
Familiarity in the imagery,
replaying quickly, now becoming
so slowed

Confusion, while defining this
revelation of realization
My presence here; decided, not
giving it much interpretation

Choosing to exist, bounded, to
the places I continue walking
Endlessly losing visions, the
blank spaces in my head begin
blocking

Everything, everything I know,
for just a mere second
A fraction, of recollections,
in limbo on this god forsaken
planet

I recognize my existence as I
inhabit myself back from 3rd
person
Come back home to yourself
Come back home to your mind's
prison

Testing my ability to write
coherently and consistently
Often times what makes sense
to others, doesn't quite make as
much sense to me

Put me on display, almost as if
I'm born to live inside the circus
Caged, where everyone can see,
and almost significantly without
a purpose

Look at me, what is it now that
you are seeing?
Is there something beyond my
transparency that isn't seen by
others quite as visibly?

Unavoidable, it is right now, but
in the future it might not even
be so
I have the essence locked within
me, let me free, let me glow,
please just let me glow

Things are made out to be
different than they seem
While shedding light on the
situation, maybe you'll catch the
truth in what I gleam

Far from devious, I hope you'll
get a taste of what I actually
mean
I'm nothing like they are
painting, or portraying, this
mirage of what they want to
think

Right now, I'm in my bedroom
laying conflicted - on my
stomach
Trying to process between the
rational and the transcendence
of this nonsense

There's that part of me that can't
help but wonder what lies below
the surface
Only I know, and somehow
people have still taken it upon
themselves to draft other
narratives

Thinking about what others
might have brewing
Keeps me hyper-fixated on
the madness that is rapidly
misconstruing

My intentions, motives, the
person truly bound from inside
me
How they'd make me out to be
something different than who
they've always known of what's
true, you see

Conflict is inevitable and demise
happens on its own
I hope the people envious of my
shine, don't knock me clear right
of the throne

If they try and succeed, I'll have
to figure out how the rest of me
will still grow
But I'm hoping for my own sake,
they'll leave me be and throw me
yet another bone

I'm sick of feeling stressed,
deprived, and most of all
worthless
Sick of thinking of the way my
name spews from their thoughts
outside of their lips

She looks in the mirror with the
same feeling of disappointment
Eyebrows furrow as the day
winds down to a close

The shower water is running,
she's preparing to jump in
But she can't cease criticizing
the skin she wears loosely on her
bones

How does her stomach always
manage to look like this?
Despite exercise and doing all of
which she's been told
Why has the gap between
her thighs begun to close and
comprise?
All she's ever tried to do was
grow in as far as she could go

Another lesson, she appears to
be learning
Sucking in, before she even
removes what remains over her
torso

Comfort is a desire only met
when paired alongside hate and
yearning

She makes sure to brace herself
for a flooding of harsh blows

It doesn't ever seem to end; nor
does it ever seem to slow
She's intoxicated in demise and
fixated on noise which screams
at her she's nothing
Nothing more than the heavy
girl, she always was to others
when she was younger

When they'd point fingers at her;
and remind her
Remind her
That nobody wanted to pick her
cause she was fatter

The tiger stripes on her hips,
make her feel quite literally sick
But at least once she gets out the
fog will mask her reflection from
being seen

Until the next instance, the
mirror invites her in again to test
the waters
She'll prepare herself for what
always seems to feel like yet
another disgusting shower

When joined by these voices
living in my head
Knowing what I think, often
times, becomes difficult to
understand

They introduce themselves,
promptly - while in passing and
on their way to inhabit me
Chaos ensues regardless of their
reason, approach, or actions

Sifting through the thoughts, of
what thought processes exist in
this moment
I begin to wonder how much of
what I attempt to express here
makes sense

A world one has to live to ever
fathom a mind of this kind
I've found it's easier keeping
most of what I've described now
to myself

Silence all around, while in the
physical and while gazing down
at my feet
Mental volumes blast from
inside my head, preventing
reality itself from being heard

Inaudible, I can only emphasize
their abundance to me at this
time
But unfortunately, can never
make out a single word when I
try

Combined with my feelings of
being both worthless and empty
I question how my thoughts are
even able to get to me

Not in the way, mine overwhelm
or leave me depressively thinking
Instead, how is it that I hear
mine among the others which
are speaking?

How do mine always manage to
reach me
When a tidal waves of others,
evidently, never fight hard
enough to ever be acknowledged

Am I something worth saving?
Trying to help, see, maybe they
could be?
Luckily, I also hear you among
the shouting from inside me

Lacking, in concept
Between the dry heaves and
sadness
Equilibrium, abandoned
When a landing could not safely
be granted

Aimlessly, combusting
Bouncing off the interior of my
skin's walls
More settling than collapsing,
Inflicting harm, or ending it all

Disruptive, this whirling
My stomach's spin cycle
tumbling on high
Can't seem to bring myself, to
consumption
Or allow myself any reasons to
get by

Troubled, by possibilities
Latching hopelessly now to
paranoid fixations
My thoughts cannot help but to
drift here
Surely damned if I stay or
damned in all other directions

Inability, to process
Beyond what others manipulate
for control
Far too much at stake today, not
to consider
The downfall of me now

Is this all a nightmare?
Reality dressed grim just to play
the role properly
I'd rather wake up and be
gasping
Than be running sleepless and
on empty

Unknowns to announce
And to lay out for everyone in
the open
A room, superiorly contained, to
expose
Propositions and motives
deceptively spoken

Time, falling away from me
Speed like light, in seconds I will
be there
Overflowing with anxiety,
confronted
Hoping the outcome is not
exactly as I fear

Held tightly by fixations
From at least one direction,
somewhere
Decisions begin making
themselves for you

Chemical perceptions, with the
most control
Guidance, which led you here by
the hand
And an inability to unlearn
what you before had not yet
experienced
These become the life that's
known

Necessity, in this process
Slithers between the bumps and
grooves in my head, as always,
moving incrementally

Slowly, it's prevalence spreads
more than had been initially
anticipated as possible
Parts, previously unknown, are
unveiled and displayed on all of
my brain's walls

Realizing, in this moment, how
the thoughts of implication grip
and dictate what it is to truly be
They can't help but always stick
unavoidably to me

Acceptance remaining present
in my reality does so all while
also choosing, at times, to drown
myself momentarily

Reflection, reminding me
the expense that comes with
allowing anything which contains
substance any amount of space
to hold or permanency

Contributions, which create
the lack of control we gravitate
towards again, after what we
love must exit
Introducing new desires,
tendencies, mirroring less
satisfactory ones, though still
held as next best

Addiction cannot help but exist
When there are infinitely many
reasons to obsess over what
occupies each of our cortical
sections

Manifestation of existence,
washes over me, constantly,
reducing my will for change in a
matter of seconds, abruptly

And most especially when
having what is wanted, isn't
possible

Hooked, what has me now and
is equally not meant to be at all
Confirmed, as they are stripped
from my memory - vacancy,
supposedly serving only to
provide more clarity

Destructive persuasion, close by
and which begins nudging my
dominant shoulder
Predispositions, using their keys
and turning knobs for passage

They assure me it's well within
me, apparently
Battling, me vs me, and
somehow not quite successful at
winning

Progressively lifeless
As I drag my feet forward

Without pride in this
My ability to find purpose
Starts dwindling shorter

Severed mind ends split
While I'm devoured amidst

What life just is
Priceless lacking bits
Fights I miss, commit
Or bliss to stick
Wrapped and stripped

Less and less meaning in why
I let myself get caught in it
Meaning nothing, admit
Controlled, twists
Now constrict
What my habit is

Of playing into
Darkened rifts
Reality, mixed
With paranoia best avoided

While I try to make the shift
Quick, fast and swift
Mental states repetitive emit
Endless shit
Telling me to stop
But only when time permits

Over and over
Cut the power

I'm sick of it
Admittance quick
Despite hatred of the game
I can't fucking quit

I mention this
As nothing is really changing

Trapped within the fit
Unable to exit this
Behind this mind, my kind
Which spits the shit
The world, exists

Never ending
It keeps going and it spins
Days dangling by threads

Feeling emptiness
Hollowed wrists, contain what
Could fill these pits within
Emotions drift

A place my mind has not yet
gone
Is where I see others around me
trail off

Drinking, to feel
Chasing liquor soon with water's
appeal
I can't tell how far gone I ever
truly am
But I like to think I have some
method of control
Not completely
I feel okay enough to stand and
not lose sight safety and life

Around me, I see my friends
drink to drown
Barely able to stand, speech
inaudibly coming out
Consuming, it appears
It's hard to really view it could
be enjoyable
It looks like torture, actually
Alcohol, liquid puppetry; my
friends are slowly pulled by
strings

Exhilarating, prepared to cut
myself off once I'm running on
a hundred
Looking around, the ones
around me continue going
Unable to keep count, spiraling
into their belligerence
A desire to be incoherent?
Am I supposed to believe that's
really the reason they do it?

Easier to picture
That I'm crawling under skin

Someone who's invading
And is harder not to scratch
once your bit

Swatting away, shooing
Am I really somebody you could
love?

Overthinking, life and all
Could I ever be someone that
you trust?

Obsessing, over whether
I'm worth more than surface
level tastes

Sentences harder to decode
When tone is lost in word
compositions and strength

Devaluating thoughts
Writing this between sleep, half
awake

Without ever really knowing
How to think or what exactly I
should say

Can't decide if I'm overbearing
Doing and asking far too much

If conversations are enjoyed
My mind tries to silence all this
doubt which is felt

Shriveled, I'm so tiny
Seeking comfort and, as always,
I'm so needy

Wanting nothing more than to
speak
While feeling like I ask too many
questions lately

Hope

Sun beaming down, not a cloud
in sight
Frustration currently consuming
my once blissful mind

One thing after the next, come
on give it a rest
Can't this game of life let off,
please get off of my chest

Panting, playing, the pups are far
from phased
Sitting back, I watch them race
through this backyard of a maze

Hungry, I'm snacking on nuts
and cheese – the perfect supply
Take a break, a deep breath, and
release - hey, the days not yet
complete

Destruction follows passion
Can't I just have one without the
other?

Reflections which are ours, yes
But still mirror versions that are
like them

Trying so deeply to precede
them
And yet the paths align so
similar

You say our differences
complement each other
But that's only when we're on
the of best terms

I'm emotionally expressive
More often than not, you're
verbally disturbed

We hold each other in bed at
night
But during the day it's not always
easy to be near

I'm fighting demons I had no
will to challenge
And I thank you for that each
and everyday

Meanwhile the ones that lie
within you
Are ones we're both inept to
tame

Finding solace in my mind and
learning to accept the version I
am now

Becomes a struggle when I
speak to you
I latch onto my inner child

You remind me to hold onto
your words
Regardless of the tone in which
you present them

But I can't help but feel the pain
you project
Isn't something I shouldn't also
be taking personal

Some moments it feels like we're
losing touch
But you always find a way to
ground me and hold me close

We're only as strong as we're
willing to be
And today is not the day I start
losing hope

Presenting the words inside, as
my mind chooses to present
things to me
Always fixating on how to
execute them or whether they'll
land with others the ways I see

Contained, within my minds
frame, are perspectives I've
longed to share outside myself
But without the consideration
from others, ever, they've
become voices I am unsure how
to tell

Deprived, in many ways, it feels
like I've been through things
well beyond my years
Somehow the shame, agony, and
guilt have become impossible for
me to drown out

On the brightside, I got out of
bed this morning, can see, and
can feel the pulse circulating
through my bloodstream
That has to at least count for
something, right? I'm here,
breathing, awake, but most of all
still living

Treading slowly, I drag my feet
back and forth throughout this
empty house
The smile I wear for others, is
easier to wear upon my face
when I'm not alone, within

I've become complacent in
this routine I live, as if living
neutrally isn't something good
enough on its own
Doing more than I ever dreamed
possible and yet the work I have
left continues to never feel it's
ever done

Visions of me standing over that
ledge again, are engraved here
though I wish they'd leave
Feelings of pain, overwhelming,
like it only just happened to me
yesterday

I wish I understood what it was,
at that time, my eyes were seeing
that I couldn't
What the hell my mind was
thinking, that taking my own life
could really help me escape this
madness

The beginning of the end, I
can reflect now, and be thankful
others encouraged me to back
down
Emotions, which only served
to deconstruct, what within me
should have made sense anyhow

A loss, in ways, because I'm
critical of my shortcomings and
what I've never been strong
enough to accomplish
But also, a win, a great victory,
that I could take the reins and
not let the impulse dictate the
path I walk on

Arms stretched wide for anyone
willing to embrace or even hold
me
Ears open and ready to listen to
anyone willing to approach me

Needy, but needless to say, I've
always needed others to support
me
I want to be the one that matters
most this time, and not give
people more reasons to desert
me

No longer willing to equate my
worth to assumptions drawn by
those who once told me they
loved me
Learning to accept I didn't
deserve every hand I was dealt
and it's okay for me to fold some

So much to give and often, not
enough to satiate my minds
hunger to let others in, to know
me
I want to share what I've kept
in all these years, but where do I
start? What is my story?

Do I start with what light has
been shed during all these years
of darkness?
Do I start by recounting each
moment, that always made me
feel so very small and so much
less than?

Much to be said, though it's
always been difficult to know
who will ever take time out of
their day to listen
Do I start with the flashbacks
in my mind, that remind me I'm
still haunted?

Trying to remind myself today,
in moments, how capable I am
of spitting out these words
How it's okay to let them roll off
my tongue, and not care how
others choose to receive them

Time spent, far too long,
focused on how to describe what
my mind's so desperately seeking
And yet, I still manage to a find
a way, better than most do, to
articulate my own meanings

Free for all, a mental release, at
the greatest of capacities
Parts of me can't help but
backtrack, what is meant by this
new process, see

Today, I let myself recite the
lullabies, I previously preferred
to trap and hide
It's my turn now to say what
inhabits and invades my sweet,
sweet little mind

Cliff hangers, though less
desired, give the audience a new
meaning towards something
more
A chase their eager to run after,
that it seems any can afford

I leave here, only a few of the
many thoughts that wish to do
marathons inside me
Crazy, they can feel and most
certainly be, but I'm not
ashamed this time, I won't be

Take a trip with me, please
You surely won't be disappointed
There's some joy to be had on
this ride, too
All I can promise is I'm worth it

Teaching
Myself, how to love life again

Comfort
In my skin, when I'm alone

Smiling
To mask pain, which all around
I feel

Trudging
Onward, regardless of what's
known

Longing
To walk these trails, alongside
you

Missing
Energy released from your soul

Living
With what, can't reasonably
change

Lifting
More, than I thought I could
hold

Sun rays
Beam down on what sadness
here brings

Spirits
Ring loud - inside echoes, which
dream

Ripples
Take breaths between each tidal
wave heave

Positivity
Though it often, doesn't actually
seem

Branches
Give support from trees as they
lean

Desolate
In loathing, humbled houses
now see

Rustling
There's comfort in the
whispering of leaves

Outdoors
Loving myself the ways I should
be

Not yet natural
Affirmations are pending, in
progress

Whispers remind me now, I'm
worth it
And surely matter, they promise

Learning to alter, my sadness
Ongoing apprentice, future
horizons

This voice inside has grown
stronger
Clouds have parted sunshine
glowing brighter

Assertive, it protects me
And influences habits which
once made it harder

Supportive people surround me
In their flesh, with great honesty

New rooms constructed
Deflective, this dam prevents
bad leaking inward

Though not perfected quite yet
Maybe one day, I'm hopeful I'll
master

Loving myself, who I am
Diminishing all I've known to
this period

Ready for beginnings to show
me
What makes life a thing really
worth living

Basking blissfully in a hurricane

The end could be near again
But somehow, it has become less
deafening

I've started dreaming of the
shadows these clouds bring

Sleet slowly sliding down the
window pane
Losing reasons to stay dry as
each day passes

Stripped of warmth, drenched
from head to toe

These petals hang on for dear
life
Waiting for the warmth they
need before choosing instead to
fall to the soil

Somehow I'm here and dance
willfully as each droplet falls

Drifting along with the breeze
It tries to carry me away
even though the rain feels so
sensationally cold

Myself, just a sorry excuse for a
human
My life, on a constant pendulum
swing
It means too much for me
to quit, but is this the right
decision?

These rose-colored shades blur
the worst of intentions

Everything looks peaceful and
beautiful
Left relying on hunches and
whims even when the sky looks
grim

The thrill of my impulses
and the happiness the storm
continues to bring, excite me

Defining the only purpose, I've
yet to find for living
And wanting to feel a downpour
on my skin in the Spring

A reflection of past decisions

Reminds me my better
judgement isn't something to
ignore
Though it certainly does make it
harder to stare back at who I see
in the mirror

When was the last time I really
thought about how my actions
might impact others?

Is this only benefiting myself?
Am I being selfish?
Am I doing what is best or
relying only on what feels better?

It's hard to really say

But I don't have regrets today
I want nothing more than to feel
the rain on my skin and not feel
ashamed

One day the sun will make its
way back through again

Until then, I'm prepared for
what the weather here may bring
Any chance is better than
nothing, and definitely a chance
worth taking

Mental release, attempting to
speak for myself
Outside I whisper but internally
I yell
Give me one good reason I'm
worth anything more
Than empty words spoken and
tears on the floor

I wish to be in a place I cannot
yet reach
Life constantly dictating and
directing my speech
Projecting my downfall and utter
defeat
My jaw grips tight on the
pavement, under their feet

This isn't over, this isn't over
until I goddamn say so
And it won't ever be unless it is I
who decides, no

Try to paint me black or pin me
to the ground
Telling me what I grasp isn't
something allowed to be found
Rendering what I love as
something I can't have around
All I wish, to speak, is even a
sound

Tomorrow, I'll rise with
vengeance, and I'll stand
Wanting nothing more, than to
share the back end of my hand

To be the person I dream, not
just something conjured
I hold onto my emotions for just
a little bit longer

Deceptive liars, who don't know
what I've been through, those
cowards
Regurgitate your opinions,
eat them, as you're spiraling
downwards

To get to where I am, I really
had to put in great effort
Monopolizing on pleasers,
rubbing their noses in dirt

Fighting against currents, though
it was never intentioned
Nor was the love I found,
anything I ever can mention

Sitting, confused and
heartbroken - meant to work in
my benefit
Newly defined, conquest to
which I'm not giving up yet

Worthwhile, rebel, I continue
what I definitely shouldn't
Because if you stood where I do,
there's no way that you wouldn't
Out of mind, I am but
forgetting you - I couldn't

Enduring blows and all this pain
if it means
Beside you I'll be, in the end,
winning

Love, which will be mine,
confident I am
In time, with you, when our
future begins

Calm, no longer crying
Subtly hearing the comfort, I
would be receiving on the other
side, within me

This is only a time; it's not going
to last forever
For now, I must muster the
strength and courage until I am
able to walk across the bridge to
get there
I can get there
I will get there

The time just can't come soon
enough
Love waits for me at the end of
all this and isn't anything I will
ever have to ask for
It just is

So, refreshing, that is
To be wanted and not required
to give a pitch to anyone else
why I should be selected

I'm not competing with anything
Love, I long to reciprocate
Although I still hold care for the
present position I am in on the
outside
It has never really served me and
never will

Losing interest in investing
towards expectations which fall
short, too
I'm prepared for this part of my
life to end

There are many reasons why
this recent discovery matters so
much to me
A wait worth a decade or even a
lifetime - I'm sure of it

There's no use in settling for less
than
Lucky, I am, that while not even
searching - this is what I was
able to figure out

Chapters open and close all the
time
Books of love, however, will
write themselves and keep going
- I know this

Thankful I have learned more
about my worth along the way,
thankful for the unexpected, and
also thankful to have found this
truth in spirit, in the process

All alone, it states, but am I ever
actually?
I guess it all depends what lens
you are using to look at it

Aching
Relief reduced to something
nonexistent
Balancing act between the back
of my neck, eyes, and forehead

Lying flat
Switching angles, all of which
have previously been attempted
Hot to cold, cold to hot
This suffering, persists
Throbbing and never ending

Obstacles, heavy
Writing, a challenge when facing
interference
Frustration, when I want to put
words out but can't determine
how to hear them

Giving up, last night
My mind clearly, couldn't
complete its mission
It's morning now, 8am
Reflection spills hours later with
a vengeance

Overwhelming, debilitating
Feeling so fucking insane
Crashing, through the guarding
rails; my brain breaks out of its
skull cage

Irritable, from delays, I must
sustain and control my mind
I want to take back what I can't
change and carve it out with a
spoon behind my eyes

Dreamed ideas with variables of
verbal ammunition
Gifting me excitement
Awakened, to the opportunity
escaping before I even got the
chance to write it

Defeated, briefly
Recalling things fresh, off the
top and from scratch
Something is better than nothing
Even if there's only a handful of
things I might add

Hieroglyphic mysteries
Engrained inside my head stone
Utterances
Of what difficulties, diffusing, I
experience while struggling

Pain, ongoing
I want to say, like what, 4 to 5
days and counting?
Pain, I've had enough of

Would rather suffocate or have
my head ripped clean right off
me
Acetaminophen, indulged
No interest swallowing more
than I have

Nothing's helping
Sleep, dulling
Aggravated, hurt
Waking angry, waking mad

Water, chugging
Immobile, though trying to do
something
Concentration, straining
Wanting peace, so why aren't any
of these things working?

Lucky, I found some words
Indeed, I did - piece by piece
Relaxation, coming soon
After treatment, I'll partake in

These distractions from life
Minimal stability, I do have
Conclude today's mental release
The circumstances, not entirely
so bad

Difficult times call for more
motivating songs
I have to keep treading
Pick my feet up, come on

Down in the slumps, I still
somehow stay subconsciously
strong
Doing as I should, I drag this
vessel I'm in, at its will, down
the halls

Suffering, I'm suffering through
everything right now
While managing to stay busy,
even in times when nothing feels
fulfilling or at all amusing

Something? Find something to
get me through this tragedy
Running out of options with
surprisingly many in front of me

How do I construct positivity
when it's chaos in here?
When the voices within me are
all that are close, all that's near?

As everything around, me
is spiraling and extremely
overwhelming - how do I look
around at the mess and stop
letting it devour me?

I know I'll get through this
It's only a time, it's true
I repeat better phrases over and
over, until I'm convinced by the
view

It's up to me to change the
rotation my mind's axis is sitting
on
I'm never alone and can't ever
stop working, I know

Halt, step back, observe, then
proceed
Mindfully, I have to ease myself
out of this uncharted sea

Tidal waves crashing, it's time to
focus and pace out my breathing
5 then 7, my anxiety, controlling
me temporarily and losing its
grip

I guess I forgot it's me who's
seeing things for a second

A moment of silence now, while
I gather my thoughts Except
my mind is on 100, constantly it
talks

Over me, about me, and most of
all unapologetically
I can't seem to grapple with
the growing pains and lack of
other's sympathy

Or empathy? Who knows the
right usage at this point Either
way, I prefer it
Not relying on the will of others
to have common sense in this
joint

Thriving, I thrive under stress
in new environments though
typically watching them eat away
at the flesh, my bones natural
covering

Skin, the sheets of fabric which
contain me; hold me together
from within even at times when
I'm not asking

Seeping, the plasma is seeping
out my pores; I tried to wrap
them tight and closed but the
sores keep oozing out below

Process, like progress, but
one requires more effort and
acceptance than I have left to
utilize this instant, right here, in
the present

A bit more patience, too, I'd add
because my speeds of processing
could use progress
Still adapting with space and
time now to manage my
cognitions and my conscious

Repetitive, I know, but I'm
sure to get things hot and spicy
as I spill them out my head,
outwards and in writing

Psyche, imagining how to
freestyle out loud once more
today but attempts haven't been
made - maybe in the evening

Instead, I spent time listening
to music while driving, familiar
words pour out my mouth and
I daydream of when I can sing
them back to you loudly

Funny, that it's easier to hold
on to what inside my head has
already been memorized rather
than expel what my mind's
always going through

Aside from a lack of certainty
my brain's tears keep streaming
from my eyes - storm clouds,
brown, but in dark skies, up
above she still cries

Suddenly, conjuring sentences
with purpose but always
releasing them in ways that make
less and less than half the sense

Pursuing, this vision, excursion,
rapidly consuming my being and
my reasoning

Somehow, on the move my brain
constantly cycles and continues
to keep thinking

Is what I'm saying taking? Do
you understand the rhymes that
I'm making?
It would be great if for once I
didn't have circle back to explain
them

For one special person, though,
I promise to always say back my
phrases

I don't mind repeating if you're
listening

Only wishing to hear things
twice so you might learn how to
feel where it is they come from

Matter over mind, mad hatter all
the time
Tripped and fell down another
rabbit hole but maybe I'll be fine

If I quit today or quit tomorrow
I still wouldn't fall in line
But if it wasn't obvious to them
I am one heck of a kind

Maybe they forgot who they're
talking to, come here now - look
inside
A little curious, delirious, and
just a pinch sublime

Tomorrow they'll be sorry
because they under estimate my
type
Nice smile, bright and large, but
I surely bark back and will bite

Today, a walking mystery I woke
up and sipped some tea to get
through
Give me the chance to prove to
them why they should follow
and let me lead, too

I wish to seek out all it is I love
but notice opposition
Minutes, seconds, hours, days
pass by but I don't ever give
them permission

To order me, step on me, or
make me feel more than most
uncertain

Because what they didn't realize
either is I'm a method thinking
person

Individual, and of course just
right, they'd never see it coming
Don't ever try breaking down
what inside keeps this engine
humming

Moving, with full momentum
and while increasing to top
speed
Delivery, they'll cut open the box
to the surprise of which is me

Never stopping, ever, when
I have my eyes set upon my
pathway
Want a glimpse?
I'll show, but only to ease their
mind and guide it back to bay

Merry, jolly, a joy to most,
although it's far from tis' the
season
I'll love who I fucking want to,
don't need approval or a reason

Flow romantic and aggressive
because you've helped me see
what others didn't

Revealing highlights once
covered up within me so today
they all can't say they've never
seen it

Shadows begin bending,
And taking new shapes before
my eyes

Staring blankly, at nothing
Discoloration effects mirages
trapped from the inside

Adjusting my lenses, again
What was blurry, becomes
focused, so refined

Refracting light, then shifts
between me
As rays project through, gaps
of dismantled clouds and widen
skies

Drawn out of sulking, finally
Fighting to escape my putrid
field of sight

Essence returning back, briefly
Slow breathing, elongates deeply
from my core right to the
outside

Fingers, for an instance
Appear warmer than was
possible earlier this morning

No longer shaking from my
vices
Or hiding from internal conflict
which was swarming

Greater than this life, to be
Although not in the clear or
close at all to alright yet

Light minimizes, my shadows
Peculiar, to me, how the sun
dissolves my disarray and
flattened affect

How it illuminates brightly, too,
regardless
Reducing my chances of being
locked in the darkness I foresee

Elevating, are these horizons,
now
Clearing, weather reframes the
fate I undoubtedly envisioned
set for me

Silence, proceeding, abrupt shifts
Masked with fear that perhaps
is written clear as day upon my
face

For now, I don't have to feel,
anything
For now, it's okay to observe the
vicinity of my space

Left with many questions, still
Hypotheticals and assumptions
wreaking havoc, smashing things
in me to bits

No use, worrying now, though
Suddenly, directing their sights at
the new opponents, from which
my sorrow here emits

I don't have to go anywhere, not
yet
Nothing lost though things
were definitely gained along my
journey, since

My mind, once more, runs wild
A runaway freight train
redefining reasons not to stress,
but even more, even more
reasons for existence

Injured, hobbling, less than
naturally
I attempted to support these
damaged parts of me

Patience required, to which I am
lacking
Longing to return back to
purposeful uses of my energy

Stationary; until wings are stable
enough to return to the sky
Limited to what gravity has set
forth, reality sinks in

Time, then elapses: this,
becoming a reflection of 3
months past
Pain no longer lives or exists
beyond past injury, today

Understanding, progressions of
the healing process
Survived long enough to
seek after this, performed all
recommended exercises

I'm thankful to be free again

My attempts to make sense of
things are consistently falling
short

Slight fixations leave me longing
for what I can never have more
of

Drifting, as the days go on,
overlapping somewhat in
between

Hints of doubt won't seem to
leave
Continually, I read into
everything

I wish I could keep up with you;
but something stops me from
catching up

I have to do this for me and
somehow my mind convolutes
it all

What I should do and what I
want to, start tangling together
into knots

Am I overbearing, in too deep?
Maybe I should stop?

I've tried reassuring myself more
than once or twice, what I'm
doing isn't wrong

Helping myself, you led me here
Venturing outside the lines to
which we were bound

Should believe you wouldn't say
anything, if it wasn't truly how
you felt

Assumed your actions would
translate differently, I'm
conflicted but also so glad they
didn't

Is it the right time or am I
someone who would be easier to
avoid?
I like to ask myself these
questions
Hopelessly, wound up;
Romantically, paranoid

As I put more words into
existence, they trail off until I'm
able to hear from you another
time

Make efforts to remind myself
you'll see things at some point,
once the rotations have all cycled
through

Just need to start finding more
meaningful things to do to pass
the time; continue on with my
efforts

I have to quit getting hung up on
what's minor and taking things
so personal

Spend my spare time cycling
through songs that lead me back
to the moments with you I can
find

Waking up to unexpected
responses, ignites the hope I had
to feel something inside

I hang onto your subtleties,
which I draw from what I don't
believe to be coincidence

Parts which fill me up, almost
immediately, then trickle off
until I'm back to feeling low
again

I love when you share pieces
of yourself with me because I
honestly care for you, deeply so

Smile stamped upon my face
anytime I get the opportunity to
see your glow

Your instincts were right to
notice I get something out of
this attention

It's only yours I've been wanting,
though, which I have neglected
to mention

Tried denying to myself it's true,
but I've loved each moment
you've been able to feed me

Imagery less vivid in ways, not
for the best
Sadly, life can't help but continue
to be fleeting

Ways you speak, even in the
simplest words, are all I really
have the ability to hold onto

Pressured conversations, due to
timing, I'm just glad you made
the first move

I sit here thinking and wishing I
could know more, than just the
few sentences time ever seems
to allow

Try to makeshift this life back to
the way it was before you, but
also can't yet find any reasons to
either

Tell myself silence would
probably be easier than holding
on to these feelings I adore of
you

Melodies will just have to do the
job for now
Things feel too good to quit

Full of wonder, I sit here quietly
and ponder
Making do, as I always do
Hope to hear from you soon

Today, I write to my younger
self
Who relied on impulse for
control

Seeking out theft for her own
safety
While feeling envious and cold

Lying to reach fulfillment
Cheating, often without
consequences

I speak to a girl, who feels hatred
From her actions, which have
carried over to the present

Time machines not available
I'm unable to erase madness
paved

Decisions made by a different
pilot
A plane, flying automatic and
deranged

Reframing, requiring my
intention
Conscious frustration in how
unnatural this is

Child, you really set me up for
failure
And I think that's why I'm so
angry at you

Look at what you did
And now, look what I've become

I have the urge to yell, cry, and
scold
Although, only at myself

How could you be so stupid
And so deceptive to one's you
said you loved

I understand you didn't know
better
But tell me why this was the life
that you so chose

There's no use talking down to
you
You're aware of what you've
done by now

Nose covered in your own shit
If others didn't see, they
wouldn't know

It's no use trying to leave
It's almost like you've prepared
for this all along

So, at this point, rather than fight
I wish to help you dig your way
back out

Gifting you, the opportunity for
change
You may fare better, become
whole

Challenging, this hardwiring
I see the cloak of toxic comforts
which you hold

Watch me burn it, it's not
working
It's time to learn care and learn
kindness

Instead of taking alternate
routes
Try putting effort into living and
start driving

I've decided to hold your hand
I wish to trust that you want to
fix this

Hoping, innate tendencies shift
pure
Wanting nothing more than our
happiness

We no longer will be lost
By ourselves, all alone and
without say

I do not blame you
For others lack of attention,
devotion, or decay

None of this was your fault
No one tried or showed you
right from wrong

You did not cause the
destruction you see
Invading your mind and within
your home

Though it's impossible not to
notice
The error in much of your ways

Only I can forgive and accept
A past once lived which I can no
longer change

Bright and smiling
But slowly
Forgetting what even for

Easier than talking
My face collapses
Dull; feeling sore

Mind going blank
Searching for thoughts
Neither moving nor expressive

Lacking motivation
Sitting stagnant
Emptiness, fills worm holes in
my stomach

What I'm feeling
Is nothing and yet,
Somehow without an exit

Hard to place
If there's a thing wrong
Or, if maybe it's a good thing?

Unable to determine
Present emotions
Though, I don't believe any
occupy me at the moment

Mood stabilized
I guess it's not all that bad
Having moments of pure silence

Mental unrest
Observing thoughts in my head
How, in ideal, situations
Inspiration wasn't made to feel
guilty instead

Studious, striving
To understand this world around
me, much better
I wish this desire
Was not stunted by lack of
support altogether

Unattainable, I used to
Tell myself so many negative
things
Though not entirely removed,
yet
I've started growing softer it
seems

Believing my abilities, previously
Were tethered only to external
sources
I've begun harnessing, within me
What I will and do attain for
myself, often

Negating my strides in education
As I pursue more schooling,
how could I do this?

Negating mental fortitude
Though apparent and
maneuvering internal forces

I'm taking steps for myself, daily
And finally, not for anyone else
I will not be made a villain
For challenging negations of
motivation, itself

Light bulbs flickering in my
mind become frequently
dimmed
As reminders are silenced and
indulgences grow thinner, then
slim

Passions for discovering, placed
in boxes for the sake of one's
personal needs
Obligations then come before
yearning I have to progress and
succeed

Mania, overflowing - prevents
me from falling asleep when he'd
like
Propelling me to take leaps,
beyond and to even greater, new
heights

It's who I am, so why constrict
what spills from my head to my
fingers?

Unable to accept defeat during
trajectories I have to rise, warm
and which linger

I will take what I can get and
don't think it is selfish to do so
Roaming ascensions to
knowledge as I continue to move
forward and trudge through

Wishing I had a space to call my
own in the present
Dreaming of freedom and
opportunities to explore mental
worm holes, transcendent

I want to be surrounded by
information but right now life
simply won't let me
Until I speak out for changes
that constrain mental resilience
and their strengthening

Proud of the time I took
recently to acquire a notebook
and write
And, as I was told, proud I
checked in with myself and
validated my intentions tonight

Psychology at its core is
refreshing yet complex
Compiled with tools that
shape perspectives and impact
emotions direct

Reflecting on earlier patterns of
negative circuitry, I fed into so
deliberately
I now lie flat on my bedspread
with elaborately shifted
perceptions and imagery

Attendance today required effort
despite each struggle to stay
focused
Spoke to others while living
within present and separate
enrollments

Feeling proud, despite forgetting
hand sheets - incomplete and
past due
I give credit that I remembered
to show up to appointments and
speak what was true

Completing all that I need to
propel me to each set of new
stages
Keeping busy, responsibly, to
fare better and move thinking to
storage

Happiness and routine now
encourage speaking openly and
free
Lately finishing many things I've
lacked motivation to accomplish
or seize

A week missed from group and
yet I still know what it means to
use TIPP
With love and support, I
naturally commit to paced
breathing when stressed

Recalling recent moments of
participation feeling hard but not
skipped
Evasions back to resolutions that
could later help if fear like this
again hit

Mistakes like explosions, jagged
cuts made in a fabric, unripped
Hanging words out to dry,
sorting each one on the line as
they drip

Wishing I wrote more things
down, to improve processing
effectively with
Paced thinking and relaxation
though I wonder how to take
such a trip

I recognize living in the past
won't solve or change that which
has happened
Seeing clear, I'm learning ways to
progress and grow the next time
I'm collapsing

Accepting hardships at the
expense of wanting better, each
day moving onward
Hopes of regulating emotions
to think more attuned and with
courage, much harder

Taking comfort in compatibility
which continually shapes all
positivity I know
Grateful for opportunities to rise
from ashes and seek removal of
mistakes which I've shown

Together, in light and in dark,
love always is teaching and
emitting warm glows
I present only a handful of
gifted lessons enjoyed and
digested methodically slow

Tearing at the seams
Can't quite swim to the top

Edges so jagged; rough
I wind up sleeping on rocks

Trying to hold my breath
But forces pull me back under

I'd run for cover, but I'm
exhausted
And I'm not sure my legs even
remember

Another battle with myself
Shit is sure starting to get old

Who do I even talk to?
Who wants to know any of this
at all?

"We get it, you're depressed."
"It's consuming you again."

Going to war, in my head
"Get over it," they've said

Doing my best to rise above
All I want is this to end

For one last and final time
I hope to scream louder than
they can

Take each voice who doesn't
listen
And shove their head under
water instead

Losing patience to withstand this
And feeling like what I want
doesn't matter

I'm sick of drowning and crying
Being unable to swim back to
shore

All I know is I haven't lost hope
And I'm not giving up anymore

Ongoing chatter
In a void with no end

I'm tired of the voices
Living in my head

Deceptively, they challenge
All this work I've put in

Truth be told, I'm not okay
I'm consumed by this dread

Why'd I have to leave?
And why'd my freedom have to
stop?

I never pictured an empty home
Or feeling so alone with my
thoughts

My appearance, now hollowed
Eyes staring blankly at the
ceiling

It's hard to accept
That my life has acquired this
new meaning

I wish I could be out
Exploring and boundless

Living by moments, running
wild
Within and around us

Not ruminating my
shortcomings
Or battling internally with my
mind

No longer tethered to this home
Or this future close behind

I built my life here for a reason
And yet it still hurts me the most

I told myself I could do this
Life was supposed to mean more

Tried to shape the future into
What was best, what was better

But it's still missing all the love
That once made my life feel so
special

Devoid, in the words I speak
Conversations become unstable

I try to build new bridges
Somehow they never get
completed

Immerse myself in what I must
And somehow not what I am
needing

These memories will again pass
Though I wish they weren't
fleeting

What brought me joy before,
Leaves me feeling dull in this
home

As I deprive myself of passion
I crawl back into my hole

Though painful and frustrating
I'll keep working to get past this

At least my life still means
something
And I can always go back home
to visit

Relax, find composure
Take a breath, deep and slow

Reality isn't boundless
Stability helps you grow

At the center, a voice that's faint
And not quite like the others

Tells me there's no pressure or
worries
Tries to remind me that I'm
stronger

Focus on this moment
Search all ends of this home for
comfort

Paint the walls a fresh color
Put flowers by the window

Before you know it, you'll be
back there
Loving each and every moment

You don't have to live miserably
It'll be here before you know it

You're loved and you can do this
It's the little things, you should
hold

Make time to talk
Continue letting others in

Listen, be heard
Reset and start over

Help yourself like you want
And quit building walls around
you

You're taking all the right steps
Don't let hard times be what
stops you

Peaceful isn't it?
The silence which occupies your
head

You're okay, so quit worrying
This time - they didn't win

Beautifully depressed
Wrapped and constricted in
mesh

Executed with intentions
Overthinking, this mess

Days cycling forward
The world spins and stops for
no one, not even I

Keep turning over, precious time
Less chances to ruin my life

I made it through another night
I question if I'm doing this right
now

I've got to focus on the road
Even when it's harder to drive
down

I wish for a moment
A glimpse of hope or maybe
peace would be fine

Make my way to the end again
Push it down, left behind

Tearing myself bit by bit
I'll dissect any pieces I find

Don't stop now, options limited
You might wreck but at least
then you tried

Onward, keep treading
I spiral further because it's
harder pulling off to the side

Blurry, my tears stop me from
seeing
Flushed red cheeks, saltwater
eyes

Dizzier, still spinning
Emotions blending, twisting
together like vines

Was honestly doing so well
Mirages, undistinguished from
lies

Deceptively envisioned
I'll let you in if you'll be my
guide

Welcome, on the doormat
The tape read "with caution",
written invisibly

A reminder I'm not stable
The will to continue faltered and
disabled

Ruminating, I tremble
Overwhelmingly
It's terrible

I have to save myself
But couldn't bring myself to
leave these keys on the table

I want to hold onto this light I
found
It was a gift that I needed

They keep shutting off my
power
Can't see
Through darkness, I've
proceeded

Today I want to be whole
Reconstructed, survival - almost
in sight

Brought back to life, within
Shaking hands, revival tangled in
strife

I'd just like to make it out
I'm sick of loathing and hating
my life

The air, so fresh as I breath it
I slowly pollute what's divine

Beautifully depressed, I still am
Living happily, I am not yet

Wipe my eyes, it's refreshing
Tomorrow, I just might be able
do this

Lead me out, so I might rest
Proof I might be hollow, but my
soul wasn't wasted

Unable to shut off the noise
Irritation starts standing up my
arm hairs

Is this real?
Or am I just imagining things are
up in flames out there?

Are things okay?
Or as bad as mind thinks they
seem?

Am I provoking this pain?
Constructing envy without truth
or a means?

I'm just sitting here, patiently
Trying to keep my head on
straight

I'm doing everything I would do,
normally
So why does my mind feel a
strain?

Bouncing back and forth
between
Whether I should say nothing or
continue the same course, visibly

One option makes the most
sense
My only wish is the others
would live in my head with more
dormancy

Growing exhausted from
disruption
Flooding my brain with
commotion

Left sitting, waiting, and hoping
Extending my slumber and
sulking

Until life resumes, I'll be living
inside dense fumes
The goal is to not to suffocate,
if I can help it

After all, my fate is not sealed
just yet
It so happens to be one I can
choose

So take a moment, I can't forget
Change is in my hands and
today's not the day I will forfeit

Beginnings, refreshing
I smile as I look out the window

Reflection, perceptive
I watch life shift into something
feasible

Pristine, vivid
I picture myself twirling in high
resolution

Free, happy
I open my heart while remaining
patient

Alive, grateful
I learn that exploring can be just
as fun alone

Soaring, effortlessly
I muster the courage to take new
chances, though slow

Stitched, anew
I embrace my vulnerabilities as I
enjoy each changing hue

Present, in bloom
I hope thoughts of these kind
continue and hold true

Seeing grey, above
Rain dulling the skies as it
streams

Reminders transmit to my brain
What tomorrow never brings

Exhaustion and pain
Persuade me to deprive myself
of sleep

Firing straight off my fumes
Unable to figure out how to
change or think

Reality returns
Consciousness allowing me to
blink

Inevitable routines
Six feet below sounding better
than tears in my sink

Repetitive cycles
Have my mind gears quickly
turning on repeat

Steps taken to move forward
Though it seems the devil's
ready to feast

Colder, feeling down
Demons grip their hands upon
my body

Loneliness inhabits me
Darkness shades refractions,
making vision spotty

Unsure how to shake this
Corrosion spreading through
mental lines

All I know is, I'll get by
Somehow, things always suck yet
always wind up fine

2008
Back when my depression began
Recession, we moved
Home, a distant experience I had

I locked the doors to my fortress
So, no one else could enter,
inside
Sought out comforts, alone
Eyes glued onto brightly lit
screens at night

Often observing, consuming
But never quite understanding or
feeling
Silence, always listening
Lonesome, hatred started
growing within me

Wondering about these new
thoughts
If I'd last on this planet much
longer
If living would ever not be this
bad
If life could be something
worthwhile

Parents unavailable
Brother despising me the most
A disposable daughter, it seemed
Living a life she never wanted or
chose

Countless hours spent enclosed
Playing music to mask pain
Self-depreciation, unleashed
Why continue? Or wake up
again?

Restlessly seeking
To end this never-ending cycle
I'm living
Occupied by mindless scrolling
Present and future, so far behind
me

I practiced until finally
I learned to tie my own noose
Wishing my life could just end
By suspending myself from my
door with a boost

Struggling, but not enough to
quite lose all my air
Rope lacking enough grip for
this game to ever be fair

I gave up and decided maybe I'd
get back to death again later
If I could do this successful
then I could be my own personal
savior

Engrained in my head
Repetitive images at times
This first moment I attempted
to end
And take my own life

2023
Alive, and no longer ready to die

At times, though, it's not easy
To remove thoughts of suicidal
kinds